BROAD WINGS,

LONG LEGS:

A ROOKERY OF HERON POEMS

BROAD WINGS,
LONG LEGS:

A ROOKERY OF HERON POEMS

edited by
JAMES SILAS ROGERS

North Star Press of St. Cloud
www.northstarpress.com

 North Star Press of St. Cloud Inc.
www.northstarpress.com

First Edition
ISBN: 978-1-68201-146-1

Printed in the United States of America.

Cover and interior desgin by Liz Dwyer of North Star Press.

Text Set in Times New Roman, Terracotta, Silverstein, and LTC Caslon.

Proceeds will be donated to Friends of the Mississippi River, a nonprofit engaging people to protect, restore and enhance the Mississippi River and its watershed in the Twin Cities region since 1993. Learn more at www.fmr.org.

CONTENTS

INTRODUCTION:

POETRY AND HERONS

Broad Wings, Long Legs traces back to the first weeks of the pandemic in 2020. Up until that time, I'd regularly attended poetry readings in all manner of venues, a practice that came to a screeching halt with the lockdown. As I cast about for a way to remain in the literary world, I thought back to a remark by Denise Levertov that "every poet of the Pacific Northwest has to write a heron poem now and then."

Might the same thing be true of Minnesota? I wondered. An email to a few dozen poet friends revealed that this was absolutely the case. I followed with a broadcast email to a larger pool of poets. Before long I was awash in heron poems.

In fact, I uncovered so many that the project required some parameters, just to keep it manageable. One was taxonomic: though it meant declining some fine work involving sandhill cranes, sora rails, and the like, I stuck to what the dictionary calls "long-legged, long-necked, freshwater and coastal birds in the family Ardeidae." [1] That usually meant great blue herons and egrets, and a handful of night herons. Another limit was geographic: all the poets here reside in Minnesota, or did until recently. And I also

---

1 This is a good place to mention another editorial decision: although the *Chicago Manual of Style* calls for species names to be presented in lower case letters, other authorities (such as the Cornell Laboratory of Ornithology) insist on capitalizing them. In most cases, I deferred to whatever the poet wrote in the original.

gathered works by living writers only—for which I have sadly needed to make exceptions, as three of the state's finest poets, Robert Bly, Ethna McKiernan, and Scott King, died before the collection went to print. I have no doubt that there are many poets in the region who've written of wading birds and whose work I've failed to include. I apologize in advance for the omission.

These long-legged birds have spurred a remarkable range of responses. Maybe that shouldn't surprise us. The herons in these pages are watchful and attentive, and they also somehow seen to set themselves apart from the world they watch so alertly. I suspect the same traits apply to many of the poets.

It seems there is a tension in the figure of a heron that attracts a poet. They live between the sky and the water. Their form balances both clumsiness and grace. Their motionlessness seems almost meditative: Margaret Hasse is struck by the sight of a bird "fishing on the shore / in the blue Zen of stillness," and Joel Van Valin's heron stands "on stilts with / priest-like attention." Yet, after standing taut as bowstrings, other herons startle the watchers when they rise in graceful flight, or when they lunge to capture a fish.

I want to call out another link between herons and poetry: it's striking how many of the poets connect the birds to the idea of language itself. Laura Hansen describes the moment of a heron taking flight as being "Like a thought long held / and finally spoken." Jeanne Lutz, spotting a heron in her "Letter to an English Teacher," admires precision in language: "you would know / exactly what kind of heron it is / the latin gray this or the latin blue that." Su Love begins, "To the reeds and lilies in the revising river, / I paddle, seeking / A word for you." (Would anyone but a writer describe a river as "revising"?)

Other poets describe herons in the lexicon of writing. Athena Kildegaard describes the birds' shape as "runic." For Maeve Reilly, a heron is "a question mark / standing near the shore." Cary Waterman finds the trailing legs of a heron in flight to be "bone pencils / writing the weather." Connie Wanek compares the heron's bill to "a cuneiform / writing deeds." And Scott King watches as "a heron practices vocabulary, / stabbing at a meal of nouns." Similarly, Elizabeth Weir finds that the way in which an egret catches an elusive fish resembles the way in which she, as a poet, will "catch an idea, flick it and worry it, / swill it in syllables, iambs snagging."

Across *Broad Wings*, *Long Legs,* herons turn up in a variety of settings. Sometimes they take center stage. Sometimes they are peripheral to the seeming content of the poem. But they are never a throwaway part; poetry, like nature itself, allows no throwaway parts.

Herons provide an image that shimmers with meaning, or invites the writer and the reader to share in the making of meaning. They are, as Jim Moore notes, "Creatures who, when stirred, open their wings / without a sound and lift themselves into another world." I hope the work here will in some way also lift us into another world.

—James Silas Rogers
St. Paul, 2023

James Armstrong

FLOTSAM AND JETSAM

The morning beach is draped with detritus
in a sinuous conga line—delicate
cedar roots,
fir cones, alder leaves,
stray bits of driftwood
whose smooth hydraulic shapes
look like car hoods from the '30s,
scrolls of birch bark
that carry the news
from moose to moose—
a few pale cigarette filters,
a stray flap of Mylar (somebody's
birthday balloon, once),
a crayfish claw,
moustaches of brown foam.
These were flotsam
but they didn't drown—
they're drying out on the sand
like Crusoe or Jonah.
But the blue S of this dead heron
with his head in the foam,
his articulate stilts
run aground
so the small clear surf
pushes his accordion neck
back and forth
drilling at cold nothing—
is he ashore or afloat?
His feet are on dry land,
his head in the trough of a wave,
caught between dry dock
and dream.

PATRICIA BARONE

MY FATHER CONTEMPLATES HIS LIFE

Hunching beneath twenty pounds
of pumpkin seeds, he whistles
through his nose. I lug
his forty pounds of thistle mix.
Strung pie pans make a tinny racket,
to rid his feeders of grackles and jays.
On the Horicon Marsh, he frees
the squirrels he nicked then caged.
He shoots a cat with his B-B gun—it yowls
and misses a flapping osprey,
which tucks its neck and sails above
the tourist boat, nearing the rookery.
Kite-shaped swans hang, not falling,
beneath the tamaracks. My father opens
his folding chair and sits to fish
as black-crested herons descend
He casts away from them,
in the deepest part of the pool.

ROBERT BLY

WANTING SUMPTUOUS HEAVENS

No one grumbles among the oyster clans,
And lobsters play their bone guitars all
    summer.
Only we, with our opposable thumbs, want
Heaven to be, and God to come, again.
There is no end to our grumbling; we want
Comfortable earth and sumptuous Heaven.
But the heron standing on one leg in the bog
Drinks his dark rum all day, and is content.

EMILY BRIGHT

MIDNIGHT KAYAK RIDE

How many lights in blackness. Jupiter has set, the Milky
    Way winds clear as any road.

Bio luminescence streams out from my bow, eddies with
    each paddle dip. I scan
        for your brief lighted trail

                find you almost close enough to touch.
We are skimming on the surface of a thousand interactions
        a lobster creeps into a trap,
        a heron, folded infinitely still, coils for the sudden
    strike: a fish snatched mid-

                    stroke

a supernova ruptures millions of years off and yes
              I have always been afraid of
           sharks and sudden accidents.

I would not have come tonight except
        you shouldered your kayak
        down the beach and paused
            at the silent edge of water.

Down the bay, the seals roil, grumbling like stomachs.
            I keep having to remember

how much is alive. How we are alive inside it. I paddle to
    you and we sit
        night-blinded, kayaks linked
            while the ocean carries us like
            driftwood down the bay.

PHILIP S. BRYANT

LIKE A PRAYER

For L. Owen

Early last evening
I watched a white egret
fly directly overhead
I looked up at it
and carefully took aim
in its direction
with all my best
thoughts of the day
checking first
to make sure
it was perfectly lined
up in my sights
before it flew away,
yet neither a sharp
arrow nor a well placed
bullet I shot
but only one or two
good, warm thoughts
lighter than air
to be mumbled softly
as if all alone in a
dark, empty church
like a prayer,
or taking a last-second shot,
where I hope my aim
was true, and hit its mark,
as I watched that
beautiful bird fly
off and disappear
into the dark.

WALTER CANNON

SIX BLUE HERONS

Two were cast as handles on a vase
and one more on a water pitcher,
gifts from friends who like water birds;
and two little hollowed out herons,
one for salt and the other for pepper,
stand with the others on the dining room table.
My last heron, a pencil drawing
as mute as any suspended ode,
hangs over the entire porcelain flock.

When I look out over Von Hertzen Marsh,
its khaki cattails bent from winter's weight,
I'm caught by sharp sounds and swift lines of
    flight:
red-winged blackbirds, triads of geese,
pairs of ducks, ratcheting and honking,
and even one time, yes, in the early spring,
the eerie croak of a lone sandhill crane,
yet in all of that marsh I never heard
the grating squawk of a blue fangled bird.

MARYANN CORBETT

THE BIRDERS AT MIESVILLE RAVINE

When they stand in the wet
where the jewelweed grows,
their binoculars set
on a night heron's pose
at the edge of a pond
with a maidenhair frond—

When a hummingbird zooms
to a linear hold
where the jewelweed blooms
in translucence of gold,
and it hovers and floats
at the jewelweed throats,

do the sunhatted heads
with their cotton-puff hair
feel the thrumming of threads
of the numinous there
in the god-haunted years
before life disappears?

By the flycatcher's call
from the top of a tree,
are they taken in thrall
as they struggle to see
in the aspenleaf green
what cannot be seen?

In a pilgrimage made
to a rural-route park,
what is sought is unsaid.
Like the sharpener's spark
at the edge of the knife:
glimpsed, but too brief.

KATE HALLETT DAYTON

WHAT IS NOT SEEN

A heron bursts out of the marsh,
disappears in the trees, and turns away
to a splash at the river bend.

I step to the cliff edge, hear the plop,
and think I spy a muskrat
moving in its V upstream
only to recognize a log caught in the mud.

I don't know what makes the water ripple.
My body savors movement
without knowing its source.

This morning,
things not seen shape the flow.

What is missing opens the story.

CHELSEA B. DESAUTELS

A DANGEROUS PLACE

It seems a beautiful spring though I spend most of it indoors
watching through warped glass small tree buds burst into full
green,

the ice crystals on the edge of Lake Nokomis relaxing & spreading

into waves lapping the bottom of bright canoes & sometimes,

near the shore, for the first time this year, a large white heron

landing on spidery legs. An omen, I tell myself: a bird too smart
to make

a dangerous place its home & I carry that with me to the hospital.

And I think of the heron when the doctors say congratulations

you're pregnant, let's shine a light to greet your baby.

And I think of the heron when they say oh sorry it seems your
womb

is more cavern than nest & no, it's no baby at all.

What have you been feeding this thing. And I think of the heron

skimming the lake surface with spread wings—how could I
not—

as we watch on-screen the monster burst into ten thousand gray
moths.

And I hear the echo of wings in my belly. And I feel the fury

of wings in my lungs. And when the doctors tuck a port

above my breast I think of the heron disguising a large bed

in marshy grasses. And I imagine the white sheets as heron
wings.

And the whirring machines are white eggs.

And the worried voices are sunlight on water.

JANE DICKERSON

IN THE AUDIOLOGIST'S OFFICE

When he called it profound,
it was a sunny day.
The room was small, and
herons were nesting in the trees
by the flat green lake.

He showed what it meant,
this loss, holding his hand
over his mouth, speaking
in a voice so quietly
I could understand nothing.

I looked at her, the room,
foreign—head phones,
audiograms, tympanometer.
I nodded my head, of course.
I understood.

By the lake, the herons
drift cloudlike at the sound
of voices, the oars' preamble,
the rise and splash
of wood on water.

I try to speak, to find
the words to show him
I am grateful for his help,
this knowledge, no one's fault.
She sleeps, infant in my arms,

but I am with the boaters
on the lake, watching
the herons settle and resettle
awkwardly in their nests.
This is no dream.

She really cannot hear.
What wind there is
moves silently. Plumes
tremble in the tops of the trees.
In shallow water one bird fishes.

KIRSTEN DIERKING

KAYAK

Minnows flash
sudden shafts

of silver light,
frogs stutter

guttural vowels
along the shore,

you feel like life
will go on and on,

if not this heron's,
if not your own,

then all the essence
of everything

that gives this lake
its wilderness—

all the bones
that rustle along

the shore today,
all the fuel

for future flesh,
for new fish,

for perch, birch,
and the petaled cups

of water flowers,
and you, for once,

moving without
difficulty

between the blues
of water and sky,

why not
rest your mouth,

let the words in which
you think too much

spill out and drift
to the bottom.

MARY MOORE EASTER

BLUE WINGSPAN ABOVE THE DOWNTOWN POND

screams heron
to the ear that is my eye.
Quick telescope of blue in the city
gone to shore among straw weeds
that winter left.
Slight gray body, all long neck, long legs
and the orange beak that helps me
find her again, keep her in my frame.
She stalks the blond stalks for food
on the ice-out lake. I edge from the walking path
toward shore but, in a burst of wings
she swoops up—span making her huge against the sky—
and folds into the far bank, gone again.
I run full out to the breathless other side,
my speed no match on land for air's relocation.
She's still there when I arrive, cautious
time to take in what dangles from her beak,
the undulations of her long neck,
peristalsis, from fifth grade human digestion.
I see her ripple and s-curve until she settles,
satisfied at her first catch.
The feathered bib on her front stirs in the wind.
Not Mary Oliver's heavy-bodied heron
on a summer pond but my slender stalker,
a swollen reed, feather-aproned among the weeds.
I keep her in view, one eye squeezed in the lens
the other confirming her outside the camera.
My breath calms as I creep—

mustn't stumble, trip and lose her—
closer, my heart beats fast as a bird's
my heron, only mine as couples stroll by
unaware of this miracle within a glance.
I sense her moves in my body, long legs stepping
through weeds, my throat spasming her new catch,
the stare we share in the endless present.
I wait for nothing amazed at our meditation
no grief of anticipation, no coming loss,
virus dread dispersed. I want to tell someone
of this coming, share the good news,
a prophet of the now.

after Mary Oliver

LARRY GAVIN

LIGHTING OUR WAY

Love migrates like the long wandering
herons make their way south.
Remember migration
never really signals arrival,
never really arrives, it's a constant, and love doesn't
    arrive
either, a pilgrimage of sorts. It lifts and turns changing
becoming something else—a road
with no end at all. Just fresh weather pulsing
with morning. Fresh as starting over
avoiding hawks and power lines
along a route seeking safe passage
and the kindness of strangers
we are love. We move with the rhythm
of the seasons with the scent
of a full moon lighting our way: blue heron guarding
the shoreline.

Diane Glancy

Epistle From A Migrating Heron

The heron stands at the water's edge.
Its neck and head like a question mark.
The box of its body on wire legs.
It could be a construct of carboard and feathers.
Like any disciple or acolyte
it concentrates on water.
Not water
but fish moving beneath the surface of the water.
A heron stands in the shallow marshes in summer.
In winter it reads its be-spotted pages,
its notes on weather,
and the frustration of finding a fish
without a ceiling of ice over it.
A heron must endure disappointment,
insects, fireflies, while nothing happens.
It's the work of a disciple to wait
in contemplation of floating ripples.
The stiff cold wind that falls.
The stutter of hail in the reeds.
The warranty of scripture
to make inquiry with an occasional scrape, a
    squawk,
a cough, rasp, complaint, *rawk rawk rawk*.
To lift its wings and fly south
to a new water's fluent edge.

GEORGIA GREELEY

EVENING RITUALS

My grandfather built a cabin on the Crow Wing
    River,
his first new neighbor a stunning Great Blue Heron
which every evening walked the shallows stalking
    fish.

Years later it became my aunt's cabin.
Still, the heron would glide in, stand in the current,
and claim his hunting territory.
Stealthy steps, spindly legs piercing the river's
    surface.

We bought the cabin on the river from
our aunt. Now we watch for the heron
each night, wondering if he's as old as we are,
or if this is the bird my grandfather once greeted.

Sometimes our heron perches in a tree
and looks around. Perhaps he sees us,
as we watch him, while dusk settles into night.

LAURA HANSEN

TAKING THE
BACK ROADS HOME

Like a thought long held
and finally spoken
the heron unfurls its
black-tipped wings
and lifts itself up
from the inky channel
that splits the field,
hovers a second,
then skims the length
of the raceway,
the charcoal tips
of its spread wings
grazing the soughing
afternoon grasses,
each wingbeat a pulse
of our hearts, each
downbeat an exhalation.

MARGARET HASSE

COLOR-PLATE 161 – AUDUBON'S *THE BIRDS OF AMERICA*

If you, too, dream to be born again
as a bird, wouldn't you want to be
a great blue heron, rare vagrant
wintering in the Azores and coastal Spain,
snacking on shrimp while wading
on long, beautiful legs? And if

you loved your life as a human who
sheltered in a small house by a lake, you
could summer there again, nesting
in the white pine, fishing on the shore
in the blue Zen of stillness when early
morning ambers the eastern sky.

SEAN HILL

SILAS FISHING 1967

That heron yonder's
a good fisherman—
patient—will wade
and wait. But it ain't
a good day for fishing—
neither of us having
no luck—just minnows
nibbling my bait.
There he goes—up and off
to another pond I suppose—
trailing those long legs, flapping
slow and steady. I cried and cried
the day Mama died. And it hurt
me deep when my wife…when
Devorah passed. But I didn't
shed a tear. Been near ten years
and here they come
like the drops from
that heron's feet.

DONNA ISAAC

RISE

Above the dripping leaves
  below a mackerel sky,
        an egret unfurls her sails,
           lifting like a velvet curtain.

A bald eagle ascends from its aerie
      soaring above the risen river
         even with the cornfields.

In the synagogue the cantor's
  chanting, "May the one who creates harmony on
  high,"
      carries my uncle's soul
        up to the rafters of our grief.

We see his blue eyes in the summer sky.

A bright moth zig-zags
  above birdsfoot trefoil.

A hummingbird jolts into the trees
  above the garden where the yellow squash
      begins to climb the fence.

Don't all things eventually rise?

ANN IVERSON

THE UNFOLDING

I love the Great Blue Heron
nesting on my pond.
I love his stress
when the Red-Winged Black Birds
peck at his head with retribution
for his thievery of eggs.
I love how he stands up and
takes it all,
the swirling wings of tiny payback
and I love, oh I love…
how the day exists beneath his wings
and even more
how they unfold: feather to muscle to bone
to flight and that somehow
in all of it I do not matter.

DIANE JARVENPA

THERE WAS THAT EGRET BY THE SIDE OF THE ROAD

The feathers seemed tokens of the sky,
sewn in another atmosphere,
shining threads of the moon,
plumes of an infallible cloud.

And the beak, that color of yellow
seen in tropical fruit or a painting
of lemons, but softer,
an enameled day lily or narcissus.
Its elegant scissor long and brilliant
hard not to think of a master craftsman.

The legs sectioned off like the advance of history,
lean and angular stems of ironwood,
the pure dark power of those feet forking through reeds,
pushing off the bristle-rind of the marsh.

The closed eye, a perfect seam
stitched by a comet tail
under a rondo of dim stars.
Once oiled and keen to flicks of glint fish
now shut to the columns of fir above,
the crunch of white gravel below
and to my hands that lift it
off the side of the road
to a shadowy sling of weeds,
left to hold and consider,
the airy hinge and bone,
helpless silver hush
of those lustrous wings.

JANET JERVE

CONSULTATION

I sit at the edge of the lake,
every cell in my body sinking,
ask myself the big question: *Do I stay or go?*
I watch the wind pull the leaves by their sockets,
stems, nearly ready to leave their country,
when the heron lands on shore nearby.
Comforted by the heron's presence, I move closer.
Caution causes her to glance back at me.
Stay away, she says with her eyes.
Undaunted by the wind, the heron faces it straight
   on,
stands erect, eyes her desire for the lake,
scans the water for fish, and completely
disregards my need to communicate.
Feet firmly planted; the Great Blue Heron lifts up
wings up—then down, up—then down,
speaking a language all their own,
her entire wingspan back-splashed
against the blue of sky and water.

JAMES JOHNSON

THE GREAT BLUE HERON'S RETURN TO THE NORTH

The great blue heron with steady wing
beats, neck drawn in, legs stretched behind,
returns each spring to stand motionless
like a long-necked question mark at
a backwoods bar asking, *Do you have any
chardonnay?* maybe standing midstream
until the woman in the too-tight Chainsaw
Sister t-shirt clutching three bottles of
Leinenkugel's in each hand and slamming
them down onto the bar like an exclamation
to the point, *This is a hard drinking, beer
drinking north woods saloon. We don't serve
any wine whatsoever.* So the great blue
heron, chewing the frog hopper caught
sideways in its yellow mandibles, pauses
and spits it out right there on the sawdust
    floor.

DEBORAH KEENAN

BLUE HERON

We arrived carrying our usual human trouble, hoping to
    walk
Those troubles deep into the forest, hoping
To leave them there. Not as burden for the forest, knowing
All too well the forest and its beautiful indifference.
At the dam I looked left to a hidden curve of creek,
Joe looked right to the still water past the small island.
Blue Heron lifted from the curve, her wingspan almost
Touched us, and she landed on the island, bowed to eat.
Right after my mother died, eight years ago, I saw Blue
    Heron
In this small valley, I knew then my mother had left
Her exhausted body behind and slipped into this new
Winged disguise. I was happy for my mother's new life.
We've searched these eight years for one more sight
Of Blue Heron. And in our sorrows this day, three times
We saw her take flight, three times land, three times lean
Into shallow water for food and reflection. She's gone,
I said to Joe. We carried the sight of her back to our city,
Our hearts strangely stirred and strangely at peace,
Her extended wings visible against the green of spring.

ATHENA KILDEGAARD

TRANSLATION

On a rock over the water hyacinth
facing away from the setting sun
a great blue heron stood runic.
To move would have been a translation
of wings from the language of water
and stone, of coursing across
permanence, to the language
of sky, wind, clouds, the realm
of uncertainty.
  Impatient, my mind
on the tasks of dailiness, I turned away,
but hesitated (that's all!) and turned
back to stone, to white flowers,
to the heron already flown.

Scott King

TORPOR

This river carries the word, drags it along
ice-piled and melting banks, in a slow
current licking sharp edges dull.

It's spring. At least it should be now.
The river not much changed but waking.
In the silty depths just a swish or two
by tails of large, lazy fish.

Upstream, a heron practices vocabulary,
stabbing at a meal of nouns—
frog, crayfish, minnow.

It doesn't trust my shape and turns on legs
no thicker than wire and as odd as stilts.

It gathers its grays and blues
from off the river and leaves like an old
book-toting hermit who needs his time alone.

JANNA KNITTEL

FIRST KANSAS APRIL

Lilac clusters hang
under heavy air.

Heat waves flood
through prairie.

Gravel road slices
grass, stock-still

in windless air,
between blacked-burned

patches. Sun burns
dusty eyes.

Yesterday, rain drowned
the canals.

Here, each season
is a pitiless sneer.

How did the ancients survive?
Rising from reeds

a white heron
arcs into once-empty skies.

JAMES LENFESTEY

HELLISH HOT DAY IN THE ANTHROPOCENE (JULY 31, 2011)

A pair of Great Blue Herons, like sea monsters in
    funeral
cassocks, rise over the bluff, two ominous silent prayers.
This will be a very bad day, when the sun strikes the sea
like a gong. The cedars wave their rags against hard sky,
    a
humid grief in which only crows row with vigor,
    sensing
everywhere the dead and dying. Sharp-shinned hawk,
that magician, lives darkly in the trees behind, chortling
at dawn and dusk the success of his swoops. So many
tourist birds pass by, not suspecting his claws, his shriek
of surprise and delight. The jays do not like him at all,
howling nasal alarms.

Yea though I sit on the lip of the bluff, a dulled,
    humbled
observer, fingers dancing like spider legs on webs, I fear
all excess. Even you, dear reader, in your narrow room
exhaling doom with every well-meant breath. Tell me,
    how
will you spend this hellish hot day and the days beyond?
What distant life will you too inadvertently destroy?

SU LOVE

THE MOON A HERON

i

Half-full and rising, the moon a heron
Blue in slow blue. The eagle must be
—Hey—a catch!

Each day I am more handsome
In my brother's hat

ii

The great egret, too
Luminous in the twilight
Trespasses the spirit state

She stands where she has never
Stood, fishes from there

iii

To the reeds and lilies in the revising river,
I paddle, seeking
A word for you. The heron

Assesses, strikes this
Day's last, delicious fish.

Jeanne Lutz

LETTER TO AN ENGLISH TEACHER

because today the fields
are too wet to work in
I take a walk to eagle lake
and see not an eagle

but a heron
standing on a soggy log
just off the wooded shore

you would know
exactly what kind of heron it is
the latin gray this or the latin blue that
but to me

this heron is simply
the color-of-rain heron

and it does not seem to take
much interest in me
or what's going on in the water

it is so still
that the fishermen walking by
do not point it out

the heron is a faulkner-looking bird
untidy
like a half-folded umbrella

and me
I guess I'm just another eve
who will never get it right

I left his heart
broke my own

and even though I still think the apple
is the best thing
that ever happened to women

that there is no paradise lost
only paradise turned down

it doesn't mean I don't miss it

I remember all those years ago
sitting in your classroom
looking out the window
while you read thoreau to us
in your low devoted voice
I watched the nuns
hang their laundry on the line
those long black stockings
lifting in the wind

and even now
when I am no longer
that young girl
in a fluttering dress
you'd think I'd have learned
a thing or two since then
but no

I get too close
as I always do

and the heron takes off

unhurriedly

sailing languidly east

never quite knowing
what to do
with its legs

ETHNA MCKIERNAN

WHAT THE LIGHT LEAVES

How quickly light slips from the sky
at dusk—the pink yolks of mirrored clouds
in the lake sliding into runny grey,
the elongated water-twin of the aspen
snapping backward to its landbound self.
Above, the heron's broad wing-swoop streaks
and blurs as inch by inch, the natural world
sinks into darkness. This is the kingdom of sound
now, the country of enormous blindness
where crickets congregate in song
and fish arc and splash above the lake
unseen, where the forest cracks and rustles
to its own percussive tune, where every map
is useless and the gravel trail back to the car
disappears. Only the intermittent sparks
of light from my beloved fireflies,
their half-extinct flickerings
hovering like small luminarias
around the outline of my lover's hand, only
the wind-kindled lake lapping the shore
like an echo of sighs into sleep.

JOHN MINCZESKI

GREAT BLUE ON THE KINNI

Seeing me through the angelica
a body-length away, it opened in a sprawl
of wings, abandoning stealth.

Who wouldn't stop, awed by such
levitation—legs trailing in the slipstream,
neck tucked in the fluid dynamics
of departure. In the sermon of the stream,

trout, unworried by that lightning beak,
picked off emerging mayflies. Swallows
snatched them on the wing, the non-

aggression pact of the peaceable kingdom
indefinitely suspended. The world meant no
harm, and mayflies—blue winged olives,
giant hexes—through sheer luck,

still fluttered back, bodies spent,
to start new generations
like depth charges. From one, many.

And a ripple of danger around the next bend,
like this folding fan of a heron flapping
over the River Falls dam.

Rita Moe

ONLY BY HAPPENSTANCE

have I encountered this egret—
  her glare white plumage,
  her signature yoga tree pose,
  her impossible, sensuous S of a neck—
in this unlikely spot:
a holding pond
along County Road C,
a cranky, sweaty suburban thoroughfare.

If I were Mary Oliver,
there would be morning mist in this poem.
Emily would tell us what is needed for a wetland,
and revery would make the list.
Or, were I William Carlos Williams,
all that would matter is egret, water, white.

Why should I go further than I am able?
wrote William Carlos.
This is enough: a stark,
serene, moment of beauty
in an ordinary, sloppy world.

JIM MOORE

NEAR HERONS

1

With the sun a full inch above the horizon, comes
the wind. The old man, becalmed in a white shirt,
    stands
with hands in pockets before the world's freshening,
the water in the bay beginning to shrug and shiver
    under the spur
of the raw, still unsettled light. Think of them, old men
all over the world sliding on their shoes in the dark,
by feel alone. Old men who do not wake their wives,
but step quietly out on the grass or sand
and stand in a place where they can see the sun
rejoin the world once again.

2

It is my pleasure to think of the men: my need
to see them facing open water near herons,
ordering nothing to happen
in these, the last days of their lives.
Near herons who know how to leave earth for miles
at a time. Creatures who, when stirred, open their
    wings
without a sound and lift themselves into another world.

MICHAEL MOOS

SILENCE OF THE BLUE HERON

Silence of the blue heron above a mountain creek
rushing over its smooth stones and trees downed in
  lightning storms,
glittering in morning sun slanting between the dark
  pines.
Watch as he slowly disappears into the shadows of the
  breathing forest.
Maybe you were wrong about the necessity of suffering.
Maybe you were wrong about needing to go back down
  to the city.
It might be that the centuries are all the same, one
  dance
you cannot help being a part of, cannot strip from the
  soul, now
more hungry than the body. Nourishment, a small
  animal taken
out of the long summer grass into the shining talons of
  the hawk,
without words or the engines of dissatisfaction.
Wind and wild roses, freedom in entropy.
You see a trout rising from the mirror, catch another
  glimpse
of the heron reading the fast cold riffles.
You could decide not to go back to the old life. You
  could thank
the river gods, could thank the dead, knowing they
cannot hear or answer. You could just keep walking the
  translucent

shallows, against the hidden current, alone. Listening.

MASON NUNEMAKER

THE RISE OF THE HERON

the heron looked out across the lake
startled by her own solitude

she listened for the familiar call
that meant she wasn't alone

at first she heard nothing
only the splash of a nearby fish

jumping out from the dark of the lake
to bathe, briefly, in the sun's light

she loved the fish for being there
at her darkest moment

and then she heard a whisper
escape a familiar, yellow beak

then many whispers, many beaks
she looked around and again saw

nothing, but heard the growing voices
of all the herons that had come before

and realized she had never been alone
she had always been part of a siege

a group of individuals just like her
fighting to survive, to live in memory

of a single heron flying, a lighted
torch held tightly in her talons

so she rose up above the lake, a thousand
pairs of wings reflected in the water.

REBECCA RAMSDEN

GREAT BLUE

Like Artemis,
    slender neck curved taut
    beak sharp
    stance ready for swift release

Her accuracy fierce
    be it fish or frogs

For the hidden nest calls
She is airborne in
    two powerful pulls

WILLIAM REICHARD

FROM *EQUIVALENTS*

through the flatness   midwest prairie

along the freeway   chains of wetlands

weeping willow   cattail   in the dark

headlights cut   through white shroud

       *

lights catch   for an instant   a bare tree

branches filled   sleeping ghosts

  in their nests

  dozens of herons

MAEVE REILLY

A QUESTION FOR YOU

Afternoon had been plainspoken—
lake complacent
with no apparent boats to beat back
no jet skis to flick off,
just the usual concourse of birds and
    bugs,
an occasional upflung fish.

But later I looked out and swore
I saw a question mark
standing near the shore—
that friendly cursive
with its dropped thought
that likes to lean into sentences
like the man belly up to the bar
—*you from around here?*
looking to get a conversation started.

For one crazy second
punctuated shore!
and everything up for grabs.
Turned out
it was the curved throat
of a great blue heron
still-stalking the shoals.

But here now, stillness
breaks, gullet unfurls
and our mandibled hunter
scissors forth
into the bulrushes
causing little hearts to stampede
all across the hot afternoon.
I can hear the tiny thuddings
and excitements
of the coming dooms.

Question marks can do that, too,
because we don't know (do we?)
how it'll all turn out.

JOHN REINHARD

BETWEEN THE EARTH AND SKY

1.
Between earth and sky
no one knows everything
that transpires. Maybe
a non-venomous snake will take
a thousand years to slide between your toes
like god's tongue
or my own.

2.
Between earth and sky
old women bring their men
to find love and frenzy hard
together, believer and nonbeliever,
stars and farmhouse lights.
.
3.
In the great blue between
earth and sky, a heron
rises from a stream. He is absolute
loneliness
and beautiful as he tiptoes,
not on the water, but
through it.

ELLEN ROGERS

LONGING: A FABLE

From the rocks, I watch
the tide drain then chase.
Desire churns water
one way, then changes
water into froth, dreams of fog.
You scuttle over low cliffs,
crunching barnacles
who take the tide when offered.
Take sun in turn.
Take whatever comes.
Beneath loose, shifting blue
tin glints. We spot a heron
who does not hesitate.
A shiver of fish under riven waves.
Flicker. Swift stab.
Light slides silver
down her gullet.

JAMES SILAS ROGERS

ON THE CANNON RIVER

for Pat Coleman

Herons, attended only
by their shadows,
stand on low mud slopes,

wait among scuffed
clamshells and gravel at points
where the river bends,

birds alone.
Our quiet, passing canoe
untethers their blue-gray forms.

They lift
and in solemn, slow strokes
row the air, move downstream.

Without wanting,
we chase a Great Blue for miles,
in pursuit of solitude.

MARY KAY RUMMEL

NIGHT BIRDS

A night heron, head inclined, freezes, eyes intent.

Nothing gentle in this night bird who brings silence
to the pond, stops the laughing red-wing blackbirds
feeding among stones, ends jay's ululations — silence
from distant shores worn in her deep shimmer.

She turns away from me in her white gown and veil.
Old nun, round shouldered at prayer, she lifts her wings,
stares into tree visions, disappears in blue reflection.

All my life I've known these old women praying.
Now I'm one of them. Crone dreams I never wanted
live in the hollow oak outside my door.

I hear their shadow-voices, collect their spells
and verses, trade one night with its cloak
of threaded silver for another.

CHRIS SANTIAGO

TWO ALLIGATORS

One swims in a Texas lake with a knife in its head

the other fights for its life

in the mouth of a great blue heron.

+

The struggling gator's
a yearling.

Together the heron & baby gator
are like an ouroboros

with the head & tail performed by
understudies.

+

Meanwhile the knife sails around the ring

like a girl in a circus

balanced on the barrel of a cannon.

+

The lake stitches her jumpsuit out of the dusk
as quick as you can name

the fifty states & all their capitals.

You always get stuck on New Mexico,
Land of Enchantment.

What, you wonder, is the capital of
dysphoria?

+

The only lake you know in Texas
is manmade & smells like lighter fluid.

+

The heron drops
the dazed yearling
into the maidencane.

Like a kung fu
master the bird
takes a practiced step

back & knifes
its bill into the garden
glove of the gator skull.

+

Any second now the circus girl

will vault off the muzzle like a sword

pulling itself out of a stone.

+

Alligators' eyes
have two lids: one for seeing below

the surface & another for when
it has seen enough.

FRANCINE STERLE

BIRDS OF AMERICA

Bearing to distant lands
remembrance of its daring
and cool courage, the unequaled
power of its flight, the bald eagle
perches at the highest
summit of the tallest tree
near the narrow margin which edges
this broad freshwater marsh,
offering a stern eye to the expanse
below. So many are beneath
his attention—bittern, rail,
wren—until a solitary heron
wades into the slow-moving water, stops,
stands statue still as she stalks
a frog or a fish or a turtle, head hunched,
poised to bring food to her hatchlings
and doesn't see the streak of lightning
as the eagle plunges toward the folded blue,
slate-gray plumage. Too late,
the wide black strip over her eye
widens, and her pale forewings fall
when the raptor strikes, talons slicing the sleek
underside, driving claws deep into flesh.
In the rank weeds, in the twisted thickets,
in the lowly shallows of northern wetlands
when strength fails and panic rises
and awful screams fill the air,
one cannot help but be humbled
by sustenance, by the morsel
weakness has become as the ill-fated one
stretches her sinuous neck and is taken.

JOYCE SUTPHEN

ONLY NOW

If I write of Orpheus only now,
it is because I did not know
that backward look until I reached this place,
this halt and stumble in the road.

If I consider Leda and her daughters,
blaming a cloudy and inhuman Jove,
it is part book and part life.

There are words I had to earn,
saving chips of my heart until I had
enough to cash them in.

There are words I had to learn,
because nothing in my mouth
fit the thought that wanted to go out
and make sense in syllable and in sound.

It might have been better to be a magpie,
gathering words, quirky with abandon,
flapping my pied wings over the dark
furrow of an empty notebook,

or easier, perhaps, a blue heron
standing on one thin leg,
bent down to the opened page,
sifting the ripples,

Anything would have been better
than this dark bird, descending and
and rising on a song that fades
before it reaches the branch.

SUZANNE SWANSON

ROOKERY

In Minnesota, in
April, in May, to find
a heron—great
blue, green, black-
crowned night—find
a marsh, follow
your ears to yammer
and clatter and clacking
unceasing.
                    Now look
for trees standing
sentinel, baskets hanging
high in their forks
or balanced
on branches.
                    Nesting
there: young balls
of filthy down
squalling for fish
from their parents'
gullets.
                    Adults, elegant
hieroglyphs, feed—
week after week—
their lineage
forward.
                    Feathers now.
Fledglings now, stretching
into that signature

stately flight, into
stopping, a standing
stillness. Sudden stab,
surprised fish,
swallowed.
                    Rookery
behind them, they practice,
practice, satisfying now
their own hunger.
We watch,
satisfying ours.

RICHARD TERRILL

THE LAKE

after Yeats

I'm getting up soon, and going to the lake,
where my father's cabin leans toward the north,
more chinks between the logs than last year's newsprint
    could patch,
old kitchen pots on the front room floor to catch the
    roof's leaks.

I'll catch black bass after dark in the lily pads,
and each day my father will talk about hunting birds
    this fall,
and my mother will read a book and occasionally
remember dreaming. It's a place of such anticipation

as when morning lifts its dew over the grass in August
and over blueberries too small in the wetlands, never
    grown sweet,
and the bittern standing on one leg, and the loon sane as
    day.
The mosquito buzz at evening sends us indoors—
    mostly safely

(everyone knows that joke, and the holes in the rusted
    screens).
Ok. I'm getting up now, because for days I've heard the
    frogs
awakening, and the blackbirds' fine syllables, and the
    few cars
on the road hidden behind the young red pines. I'm
    down that road,

away, always away now, and looking
toward its farthest bend.

Joel Van Valin

BACKWATER

Back in the shallows
where water stills enough—
cool shadow hollows—

for self reflection,
you stand on stilts with
priest-like attention.

Do you dream of the flight—
sky-mist and stream,
that warmer shore

with its younger light—
or is it just the gleam
you're fishing for?

MARK VINZ

FISHERMEN

for Keith
Upper Cormorant Lake, Minnesota

We've finally found the time to get away,
this early June morning with a misty chill
still hanging over the lake. We're alone today,
two bass fishermen, stubbornly working the
thick weed beds along the shore—suddenly
startled by a huge Great Blue rising only
a few yards away from the green walls which
surround us. Such a majestic bird in flight,
so raucous in his scolding cries of departure.

On the slow drive home in fading light
we see the herons flying high above us
and dream ourselves back to the reeds—
their reeds—where fishermen gather and
it's impossible to know what's coming.

CONNIE WANEK

BIG ALDEN LAKE

We lived, briefly, on Big Alden,
where the river widens into the shape
of a full stomach: pike, bass, bluegills.
The mythic white pine
that once covered these hills
never grew back. They say the lumber
"built St. Louis."

Now the water's cloudy from cabin septics
like ours. Paddle upstream, though
and the water clears and grows younger.
There a heron spears a frog in the reeds,
its bill a cuneiform recording
deeds, and meals.

The heron isn't here forever
either. One cabin across the water
has its own little white airplane
perched near the dock like a dragonfly.
Our oldest dream involves breathing
underwater, and afterwards, flying.

CARY WATERMAN

BONFIRE

She's cleaned out her files,
shed skins, papers, check registers,
tax returns for the 90's,
directions for the electric waffle maker,
receipts for drugs she needed,
auto insurance stubs,
assets, debits.
She makes a bonfire of it all.

Clumps of nests in bare trees.
Birds wheel overhead,
nimbleness of a Black Hawk.
Down here ghosts toss
back and forth in the wind.

The gnats are out and they're biting.
The sky's a dreamy gauze.
Trees twirl in fall dresses and an old Blue
    Heron
flies over from lake to river.

She doesn't own much.
Only her long legs stretched out,
bone pencils writing the weather.

ELIZABETH WEIR

FISHING

A watchful egret stabs into pond weed, catches
a twisting fish crosswise in dagger bill.

Fish glints silver. Bird tosses it, shakes it,
dibbles it in water, flips it again,

until it lands, head towards gullet,
scales slanting the right way, and swallows

as I catch an idea, flick it and worry it,
swill it in syllables, iambs snagging,

until words slip into rhythm,
every trochee, sliding smoothly.

GWEN WESTERMAN

MIGRATION PATH

Standing
immobile,
stark
white
against
a late
summer
field
now more
golden than
green, a heron
seems to gaze
beyond the
windbreak,
waiting,
watching,
perhaps listening
to the songs of
frogs and locusts.
I stop
and gaze
beyond the
windbreak,
let go
of the fear,
and breathe.

MORGAN GRAYCE WILLOW

BLUE HERON CINQUAIN

Geekish.
Long-legged, long-
necked in flight. Foolish bird.
Squawking, as if I'd steal your nest.
Relax.

TRACY YOUNGBLOM

IT BEGINS

A gray fox starts, skirts
the wood, nimble among
fallen branches.

Who placed the frame of the blinking
egret, slender white line
motionless
near the swamp's edge?
A fish flashes,
the silhouette bends,
straightens.

The red breast of sun
grazes the horizon,
strains against the tides.
Light requires
struggle.
The first bruised shadows
appear, darken
the dark ground.

Morning raps at windows.
Outside the upturned palm
of the world cradles
the day: let sleep
fall from your eyes
like scales.

CONTRIBUTORS

James Armstrong is the author of *Monument in a Summer Hat* and *Blue Lash*, and is the co-author of a book of essays, *Nature, Culture and Two Friends Talking*. He is a professor at Winona State University, and was Winona's first poet laureate.

Patricia Barone's poetry collections are *The Music of this Ruin; Your Funny, Funny Face; The Scent of Water*; and *Handmade Paper*. Her awards include a Loft-McKnight Award of Distinction in poetry, and a Minnesota State Arts Board Opportunity Grant.

Robert Bly (1926-2021) was one of America's most influential poets, as well as a translator and activist. The author and editor of more than forty books, his collection *The Light Around the Body* won the National Book Award for Poetry. In 2008 he was named the first poet laureate of Minnesota.

Emily Bright writes for both page and radio. An MFA grad from the University of Minnesota, she is the author of the chapbook *Glances Back*. Her poems have appeared in *America, The Pedestal Magazine*, and in numerous other journals.

Philip S. Bryant is the author of *Blue Island, Sermon on a Perfect Spring Day*, and *Stompin' at the Grand Terrace*. His work has appeared widely, including in *Blues Vision: African American Writing from Minnesota*, and *Good Poems, American Places.*

Walter Cannon is the author of *The Possible World*, a chapbook, and has poems published in numerous anthologies, reviews, and journals. Cannon is the co-editor of *Who Hears in Shakespeare?* and *Shakespeare's Auditory Worlds.*

Maryann Corbett is the author of two chapbooks and five full collections, most recently *In Code*. Her work has appeared in journals including *Able Muse, Barrow Street, Christianity and Literature, Ecotone*, and *Rattle*.

Kate Hallett Dayton is an avid photographer, gardener, and knitter. She is the author of the collections, *Salt Heart*, and of two chapbooks, *Catalpa* and *Missing*. Her work has appeared in *Nimrod International, Flyway, Passages North*, and elsewhere.

Chelsea B. DesAutels is the author of *A Dangerous Place*, a New York Times Editors' Choice. She has received support from the Anderson Center at Tower View, Bread Loaf Writers' Conference, Inprint, Tin House Workshop, and others.

Jane Dickerson earned an MFA at the University of Maryland, College Park, under the guidance of Stanley Plumly. Her work has appeared in many small magazines and in her collection *The Orange Tree: Early Poems*.

Kirsten Dierking is the author of *Tether, Northern Oracle*, and *One Red Eye*. She is grateful for grants, awards, and support from such organizations as the McKnight Foundation, the Loft, the Banfill-Locke Center, and the Minnesota State Arts Board.

Mary Moore Easter is the author of four poetry books: *From the Flutes of Our Bones, The Body of the World, Walking from Origins*; and *Free Papers*. She has recently completed a memoir, *The Way She Wants to Get There: Telling on Myself.*

Larry Gavin is the author of five books of poetry, the most recent of which is *A Fragile Shelter: New and Selected Poems*. He recently retired after many years of teaching English at Faribault High School.

Diane Glancy is professor emerita at Macalester College. She is the author of numerous books, most recently *Island* *of the Innocent: A Consideration of the Book of Job.* She co-edited the anthology *Unpapered: Writers Consider Native American Identity.*

Georgia Greeley is an artist and writer. She writes in a variety of genres: poetry, children's literature, fiction, memoir, and essay. She is the author of children's short stories in educational magazines, including *Highlights for Children.*

Laura Hansen is the author of *Midnight River*, which won the Stevens Poetry Manuscript Prize. She owned an independent bookstore for twenty years and now works at her local library in Little Falls.

Margaret Hasse's recent poetry books are *Shelter*, a collaboration with artist Sharon DeMark; *Summoned*, influenced by the murder of George Floyd; and *The Call of Glacier Park*. Grants from Jerome Foundation, McKnight Foundation, Minnesota State Arts Board and NEA have supported Hasse's writing life.

Sean Hill is the author of two collections: *Dangerous Goods* (awarded the Minnesota Book Award in poetry), and *Blood Ties & Brown Liquor*. Formerly at Bemidji State University, Hill is now a professor of creative writing at the University of Montana.

Donna Isaac is a teaching artist who organizes community readings and workshops. She earned an MFA in writing from Hamline University. Her publications include *Footfalls*; *Tommy*; *Holy Comforter*; and *Persistence of Vision*.

Ann Iverson is a poet and artist. She is the author of five poetry collections and a graduate of both the MALS and the MFA programs at Hamline University. Her poems have appeared in six readings on *The Writer's Almanac*.

Diane Jarvenpa is the author of *The Way She Told her Story*, *The Tender Wild Things*, *Divining the Landscape, swift, bright, drift* and *Ancient Wonders, The Modern World*. She is a singer-songwriter performing under the name Diane Jarvi.

Janet Jerve is the author of the collection *Excavation*. Her poems have appeared in such places as *Beloved on the Earth*, *The Heart of All That Is*, and *Amethyst and Agate: Poems of Lake Superior*.

James Johnson, a former poet laureate of Duluth, lived most of his life in Northern Minnesota. He has published ten books of poetry, most recently *One Morning In June: Selected Poems*.

Deborah Keenan is the author of eleven collections of poetry, a recipient of the Minnesota Book Award in Poetry, and a professor in the MFA program at Hamline University for thirty years.

Athena Kildegaard's most recent book is *Prairie Midden*. She teaches at the University of Minnesota Morris.

Scott King (1965-2021) was a poet, editor, translator, and naturalist in Northfield, His collections include *All Graced in Green*, *Dragonfly Haiku*, and *Following the Earth Around: Journal of a Naturalist's Year*. In 1999, he founded Red Dragonfly Press, a fine press publisher that brought out the work of many of the region's most notable authors.

Janna Knittel is the author of *Real Work* and the chapbook *Fish & Wild Life* and has published in such journals as *Cottonwood*, *North Dakota Quarterly*, and *The Wild Word*, as well as in *Waters Deep: A Great Lakes Anthology*.

James Lenfestey has published two collections of personal essays, seven collections of poems, edited three poetry anthologies, and co-edited *Robert Bly in This World*. He received the 2020 Kay Sexton Award for contributions to the Minnesota literary community.

Su Love is the author of six collections of poetry; T*he Memoir of Mona Lisa and Other Poems* is her most recent book. Her poetry has been recognized with distinguished awards, international publications, fellowships, and residencies.

Jeanne Lutz grew up on a small dairy farm in southern Minnesota, attended the National University of Ireland Galway, and spent two years in Japan. A Pushcart Prize nominee, Best-of-the-Net nominee, and winner of the Loft Mentor Series for poetry, she is the author of *Until the Kingdom Comes*.

Ethna McKiernan (1951-2021) was the author of five books of poetry, including *Light Rolling Slowly Backwards: New and Selected Poems*. After a long career as CEO of Irish Books and Media, McKiernan worked more than a decade as an outreach worker for charities serving the homeless.

John Minczeski is the author of five poetry collections, several chapbooks, and has contributed to many literary journals. He has worked as a poet in the schools and has taught at assorted colleges around the Twin Cities.

Rita Moe earned an MFA from Hamline University. Her poetry has appeared in *Water-Stone*, *Diagram*, *Slipstream* and other journals. She is the author of two chapbooks: *Sins & Disciplines* and *Findley Place; A Street, a Ballpark, a Neighborhood.*

Jim Moore lives in Minneapolis with his wife, the photographer JoAnn Verburg. Graywolf Press published his most recent book of poems, *Prognosis*, in November 2021.

Michael S. Moos has published four poetry books, most recently *The Idea of the Garden*. He has received awards from the NEA, the Minnesota State Arts Board, and the Loft Literary Center in Minneapolis. He has an MFA from Columbia University.

Mason Nunemaker graduated from the University of Minnesota where he earned a BA in English, with an emphasis in poetry writing. He was an officer of the UM's slam poetry organization and represented them twice at the College Unions Poetry Slam Invitational.

Rebecca Ramsden, a retired nurse, is the guts behind Poets Chair, where she posts on social media about her journeys. A past winner of the Creekside Poetry Contest, her poems have appeared in *Martin Lake Journal*, *Talking Stick*, and elsewhere.

William Reichard is a writer, editor, and educator. The most recent of his seven poetry collections is *Our Delicate Barricades Downed*.

Maeve Reilly, a fifth-generation Minnesotan, lives within the St. Croix watershed. She has recently completed *The Old Way Home*, a memoir of her backwards emigration to a remote mountainside in the northwest of Ireland,

John Reinhard is the author of two poetry collections, *On the Road to Patsy Cline* and *Burning the Prairie*. He is a two-time recipient of the Loft-McKnight Prize in Poetry. He teaches at South Central College in Faribault.

Ellen Rogers's poems and essays can be found in *AGNI*, *Ecotone*, *River Teeth*,and other journals. She holds an MFA in creative writing from Western Washington University and has served as an editor for *Bellingham Review* and *The Hopper*.

James Silas Rogers is the author the poetry collection *The Collector of Shadows*, as well as a nonfiction book about cemeteries, *Northern Orchards: Places Near the Dead*. He has also published widely on Irish writing.

Mary Kay Rummel's ninth poetry book is *Nocturnes: Between Flesh and Stone*. Her collection, *This Body She's Entered*, won the Minnesota Voices Award from New Rivers Press. She taught at UMD and at Cal State.

Chris Santiago is the author of *Tula*, winner of the Lindquist & Vennum Prize and a finalist for the Minnesota Book Award. He is a Loft Poetry Mentor and a Kundiman, McKnight, and Mellon Foundation/ACLS Fellow. He teaches at the University of St. Thomas.

Francine Sterle's poems have been appeared in such journals as *North American Review*, *Ploughshares*, and *Nimrod* and have been widely anthologized. Her four collections include *Every Bird is One Bird*, which won the Editor's Prize of Tupelo Press.

Joyce Sutphen's first collection, *Straight Out of View* won the Barnard New Women Poets Prize in 1995, and her collection *Naming the Stars* won the Minnesota Book Award in poetry. She served as Minnesota's second poet laureate from 2011-2021.

Suzanne Swanson, a retired psychologist, is the author of *House of Music* and the chapbook *What Other Worlds: Postpartum Poems*. She is a winner of the Loft Mentor Series and helped to found the Laurel Poetry Collective.

Richard Terrill's newest book is *What Falls Away Is Always: Poems and Conversations*. Among his four previous books are *Coming Late to Rachmaninoff*, winner of the Minnesota Book Award, and two memoirs. He works as a jazz saxophonist.

Joel Van Valin is the publisher of the literary journal *Whistling Shade*. He is the author of a time travel novel, *The Grand Dissolute*, and a fantasy novel, *The Flower of Clear Burning*. His first chapbook is *The White Forest*.

Mark Vinz is professor emeritus at Minnesota State University Moorhead and was editor of the poetry journal *Dacotah Territory*. He has also co-edited several collections, including *Inheriting the Land: Contemporary Voices from the Midwest.*

Cary Waterman is the author of seven books of poems, including *The Salamander Migration, When I Looked Back You Were Gone* (a finalist for the Minnesota Book Award), and *Book of Fire* (a finalist for the Midwest Book Award).

Connie Wanek is the author of six collections of poetry, including a children's book, *Marshmallow Clouds*, co-written with Ted Kooser. She lived in Duluth for a quarter century, where a wildflower trail was named in her honor.

Elizabeth Weir grew up in England. Her book, *High on Table Mountain* was nominated for the 2017 Midwest Poetry Book Award. Her second book is *When the World Was Whole*, She has received two S.A.S.E. Jerome awards.

Gwen Westerman is a Dakota educator, writer and artist. She been honored by many cultural and literary organizations, including The Loft, the Minnesota Book Awards, and the Smithsonian Institution, and was appointed Minnesota's third poet laureate in 2021. She is professor of English at Minnesota State University, Mankato.

Morgan Grayce Willow has published three collections, most recently *Dodge & Scramble*. A book artist, she is one of four poets who together wrote and hand crafted the limited edition chapbook *Stitch by Stitch* to accompany the

"Quilt, Not Quit" exhibition at the Minnesota Center for Book Arts in 2018.

Tracy Youngblom has been part of the Twin Cities writing community for more than thirty years. Her most recent book is *Boy.* Her work has been featured in many journals and anthologies, and have been honored by two Pushcart nominations.

BROAD WINGS, LONG LEGS:

ACKNOWLEDGMENTS

James Armstrong, "Flotsam and Jetsam" appeared in *Blue Lash*, Milkweed Editions, 2006.

Patricia Barone, "My Father Contemplates His Life,' appeared in *The Music of This Ruin*, Taj Mahal Press, 2021.

Robert Bly, "Wanting Sumptuous Heavens" appeared in *The New Yorker*, November 5, 2007.

Emily Bright, "Midnight Kayak Ride" appeared in *Other Voices International*, vol. 41 (2009) and in *Ocean* (2013).

Philip S. Bryant, a slightly different version of "Like a Prayer" appeared in *The Promised Land*, Nodin Press, 2018.

Maryann Corbett, "Birders at Miesville Ravine" appeared in *Gatherings: Journal of the International Community for Ecopsychology*, 2006.

Chelsea DesAutels, "A Dangerous Place" from *A Dangerous Place: Poems*, Copyright © 2021 by Chelsea DesAutels. Reprinted with the permission of Sarabande Books, Inc.

Jane Dickerson, "In the Audiologist's Office" appeared in *The Orange Tree: Early Poems,* Levins Publishing, 2015.

Kirsten Dierking, "Kayak" appeared in *Tether*, Spout Press, 2013.

Margaret Hasse, *Audubon's* The Birds of America, *Color-plate 161*, appeared in *Summoned*, Nodin Press, 2021.

Sean Hill, "Silas Fishing 1967" appeared in *Blood Ties & Brown Liquor*, UGA Press, 2008.

Donna Isaac, "Rise" appeared in *The Martin Lake Journal*, 2017.

Ann Iverson, "The Unfolding" appeared under a different title in *Art Lessons*, Holy Cow! Press 2011.

Diane Jarvenpa, "There was that egret by the side of the road" appeared in *swift, bright, drift*, Red Dragonfly Press, 2016.

James Johnson, "The Great Blue Heron's Return to the North" appeared in *Text For Our Nomadic Future*, Red Dragonfly Press, 2018.

Athena Kildegaard, "Translation" appeared in *Bodies of Light*, Red Dragonfly Press, 2011.

Deborah Keenan, "Blue Heron" appeared in *Kingdoms*, Laurel Poetry Collective, 2006.

James Lenfestey "A Hellish Hot Day in the Anthropocene" appeared in *Earth in Anger: 25 Poems of Love and Despair for Planet Earth*, Red Dragonfly Press, 2013.

Su Love, "The Moon A Heron" appeared in a different arrangement in *You This Close*, Red Dragonfly Press, 2016.

Jeanne Lutz, "Letter to an English Teacher" appeared in *The Missouri Review*, 2017.

Ethna McKiernan, "What the Light Leaves" appeared in *The One Who Swears You Can't Start Over*, Salmon Poetry, 2002.

Jim Moore, "Near Herons" appeared in *The Freedom of History*, Milkweed Editions, 1988.

William Reichard, "Equivalents" appeared in *This Brightness: Poems*, Mid-List Press, 2007.

Mary Kay Rummel, "Night Birds" appeared in an earlier version in *Green Journey/Red Bird*, Loonfeather Press, 2002.

James Silas Rogers, "On the Cannon River" appeared in *The Collector of Shadows*, Brighthorse Books, 2019.

Richard Terrill, "The Lake" appeared in *What Falls Away Is Always,* Holy Cow! Press, 2020.

Cary Waterman, "Bonfire" appeared in *Book of Fire*, Nodin Press, 2011.

Morgan Grayce Willow, "Blue Heron Cinquain" appeared in *Arpeggio of Appetite*, Finishing Line Press, 2005.

Elizabeth Weir, "Fishing" appeared in *The South West Journal*, 2017.

Tracy Youngblom, "It Begins" appeared in *Growing Big*, North Star Press of St. Cloud, 2013.